~ LIFE'S A JOURNAL, NOT

THE

BREAKUP

JOURNAL

~ BREAK UP WITHOUT THE BREAKDOWN ~

TOM DEVONALD

CARLTON
BOOKS

This book is dedicated to
GTA: San Andreas

Tom Devonald is a UK-based
writer and graphic designer.
Known to his friends for his love of doodling and
his terrible memory. His main topics of interest are
psychology, design, philosophy and psychology.
See more of his stuff on his website:
tommydevonald.com

THIS IS A CARLTON BOOK
Published by Carlton Books Ltd
20 Mortimer Street
London W1T 3JW

ISBN 978 1 78097 829 1

IT'S OVER.
Your fling has flung.

The one who used to make you sentimental has sent you mental.

Your once-passionate affair looks more like the passion of the christ.

Now your frail, broken heart pumps only bad blood through your aching limbs and the world has a kind of greyish hue to it like in the Twilight movies.

You two used to be all sexy and tense together like John Travolta and Uma Thurman in Pulp Fiction but now you're more like John Travolta and Nicholas Cage in Face Off; desperately trying to remove every last part of the other one from your being even if it requires radical reconstructive surgery.

You two were an item. THE item. Now you're standing alone in the five-items-or-less line with a microwave meal, a bottle of 'Thor Power' energy-drink-flavoured-cider, and a 3 quid DVD of 'Marley and Me'.

There's no use denying it. Single life isn't really the aspirational-alcohol-advert-inspired, free-loving knees-up you would occasionally imagine in those quiet moments back in the trudging comfort of when you were tied down. This feels more like an alcohol awareness advert.

Fear not, this blip in your otherwise potentially awesome life is only temporary.

This broken heart is not a terminal affliction. You have (fortunately for you) stumbled across this book! Things are about to change for the better.

This book is your new partner.

Helping you to create a bespoke record of this time for posterity and amusement (and potentially to be used as evidence in a court of law if it comes to that).

Think of it as a map and a compass, a battle plan and a medipack. Let it be the Chewbacca to your Han Solo as we fly through this galaxy of pain at light speed on a journey to planet 'Anywhere-but-how-you-are-feeling-right-now'.

Think of it as a vibe sponge that will absorb your bad vibes and wash you with a new lease of good vibes.

LET'S BEGIN...

PART 1
THE
BREAK-UP
REPORT

The date of the break-up:  / /

How this day shall
henceforth be known:

Feel free to
share your
creations

#BREAKUPJOURNAL

(keep it clean people).

BEST day of your life

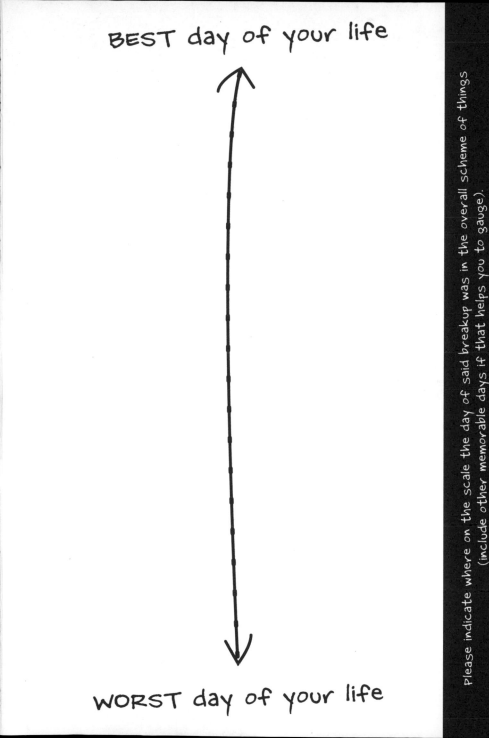

WORST day of your life

Please indicate where on the scale the day of said breakup was in the overall scheme of things (include other memorable days if that helps you to gauge).

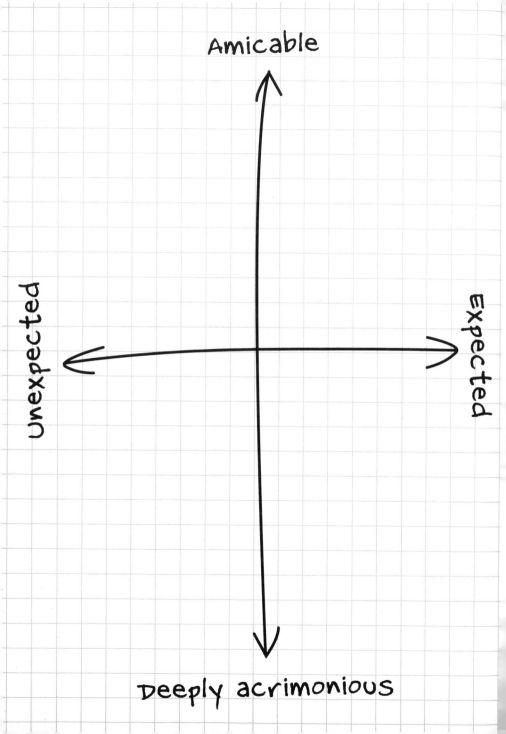

EX marks the spot

Mark the general mood of the breakup on these charts with an X

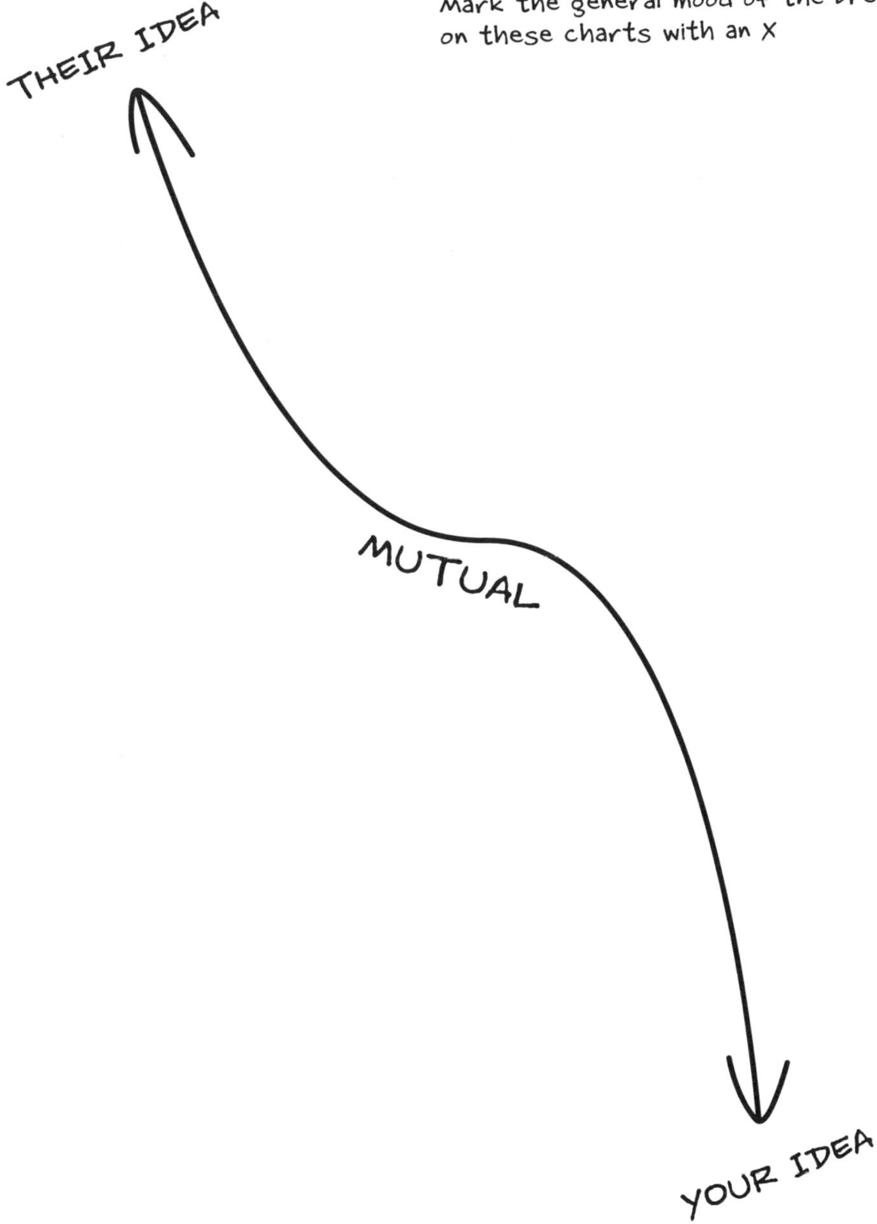

THEIR IDEA

MUTUAL

YOUR IDEA

Write your
OFFICIAL VERSION OF EVENTS
on this page

(this is what you will tell other people happened)

TIP: Keep it simple
e.g. 'we went our separate ways'
'we had creative differences'

Double tip: Practice saying it aloud in the mirror as nonchalantly as possible.

BREAKUP CLICHÉ BINGO

I don't know how to say this but...	We need to talk...	It's not you... it's me	I feel like we've grown apart
I just need space	Things haven't been great for a while	We can still be friends	I'm not saying this is the end
It's just not working for me	I just need time	It's not that I don't love you	You deserve someone better
We should see other people	I just feel like I haven't experienced enough life outside of this relationship	We've been leading two different lives	I love you but I'm not IN love with you

Put a big X through cliches that were said when the deed was being done. If you score FOUR IN A ROW in any direction then your breakup lacks originality and flair. You can shout 'BINGO *#@% yourself'.

Things that they said:

TRANSLATION:
(what they actually meant)

Now write down all of the logical comebacks and witty ripostes that came into your head approximately 15 seconds after they left.

THE FULL

THEIR
SIDE OF THE STORY

STORY

YOUR
SIDE OF THE STORY

PART 2

WAIT!

CAN YOU
WIN THEM BACK?

DO YOU WANT them back?

YES!
They broke up with me and I'm heartbroken

Write down your strategies in order of expensiveness

Free ideas:

a. Surprise them with a carefully orchestrated, well oiled, dancing flash mob singing their favourite song; then you paraglide in from space and ask them to marry you.*

b. A subtle, deep and meaningful gesture that only the two of you will understand.*

c. Making a genuine change to your clearly flawed character.

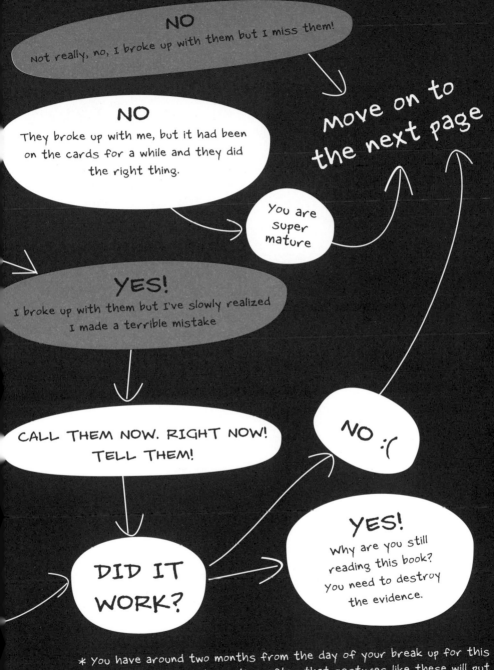

NO
Not really, no, I broke up with them but I miss them!

NO
They broke up with me, but it had been on the cards for a while and they did the right thing.

move on to the next page

You are super mature

YES!
I broke up with them but I've slowly realized I made a terrible mistake

CALL THEM NOW. RIGHT NOW! TELL THEM!

NO :(

DID IT WORK?

YES!
Why are you still reading this book? You need to destroy the evidence.

* You have around two months from the day of your break up for this behaviour to appear normal. Any time after that gestures like these will put you into the 'psycho-ex' category. At this point you should move on to idea 'c.'

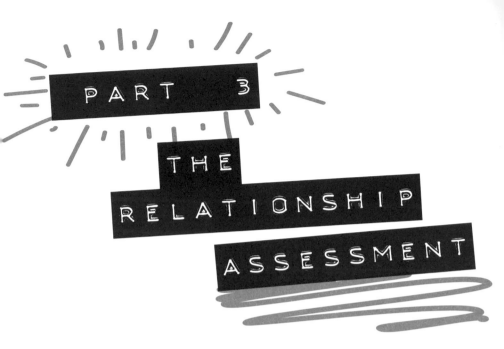

PART 3

THE RELATIONSHIP ASSESSMENT

I mean, Was it even THAT good?

The relationship
compared to other relationships

Name of relationshipee:	LENGTH of relationship: years / months / weeks / days / minutes / seconds	DEPTH of relationship: (create your own unit of measurement)

HAPPINESS
IN THE RELATIONSHIP

_____

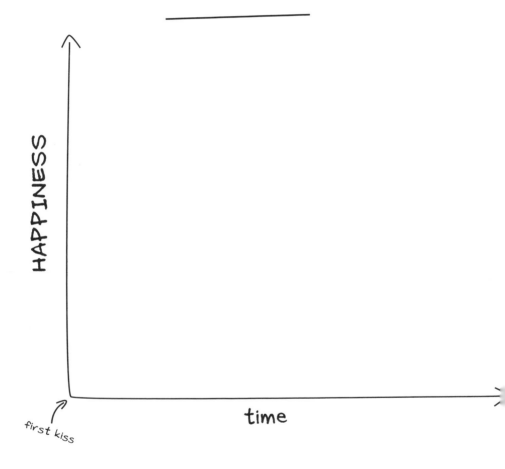

HAPPINESS

time

first kiss

Fill out these flow charts, indicating any key events in the relationship with an X and labelling them.

(Ahem...)

SEXINESS
IN THE RELATIONSHIP

QUALITY
QUANTITY

time

first kiss

Draw two lines on this chart
using two different colours
for Quantity and Quality.

KEY:

QUALITY ☐
QUANTITY ☐

Fill in this pie chart of how much time you spent together in an average week.

KEY:
■ together —
□ apart

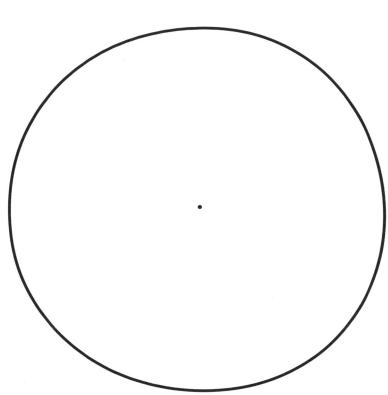

colour in this pie chart
of HOW you two spent
your time together.

MAKE YOUR OWN KEY:

☐ _____
☐ _____
☐ _____

☐ _____
☐ _____
☐ _____

what do you think you will
still remember from the
relationship in 10 years time?

what about 20?

Summarize the relationship as though it was a film and write the voiceover for the advert.

IN A WORLD ...

Was it an action, a comedy or a horror?

make your own

SPOT THE

HOW YOU SAW THEM AT THE
BEGINNING

DIFFERENCE

HOW YOU SEE THEM
NOW

Write a review of your relationship as though it was a meal and you are a restaurant critic.

what was the starter, main and dessert? what was each dish called?

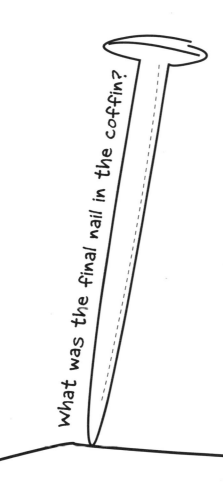

What was the final nail in the coffin?

write about them here
WHEN YOU ARE
SAD

write about them here
WHEN YOU ARE

Bitterness rating

Complete these phrases to get a gauge on how bitter you are feeling

...(if at all)

Roses are red, violets are blue, ...

All's .... that ends ....

Better to have .... and .... than never to have .... at all

All's .... in .... and ....

When life give you lemons, ...

Romeo, Romeo, ...

Lucky in ....

Frankly my dear, ...

How many lemons out of 5 would you give yourself?

couldn't be better $\bigcirc$ $\bigcirc$ $\bigcirc$ $\bigcirc$ $\bigcirc$ couldn't be bitterer

'SCRAP' BOOK

-YOUR TOP 5 MOST EPIC ARGUMENTS-

1 _____

2 _____

3 _____

4 _____

5 _____

(was there a recurring theme?)

Write down any regrets you have here:

ALL DONE?
Great, now rip out this page and
flush it down the toilet with all the
other crap that is of no use to you.

what were the best and worst
things about your relationship?

 BEST:

 WORST:

cut out this page

fold it into a little paper boat.

HMS: whatever

This is your
relationSHIP

SINK IT.

(solemnly with a sense of sombre ceremony)

PLACES TO SINK IT:
> The bath
> A river   > In a bucket of tears
> The dead sea   >
> Niagara falls   >
> A puddle   >

CONGRATULATIONS!
Your relationship
has sunk, but

YOU
HAVE SURVIVED

I'm afraid it's now time for

PART 4

THOSE PESKY

EMOTIONS

DIY

PSYCHOLOGICAL ASSESSMENT KIT

Pour some ink into the gutter of this page and then close the book to make a Rorschach test.

what do you see?

make some kind of WARNING sign here that lets people know that you're actually not really in the mood for their nonsense quite frankly

(due to emotional conditions that are outside of your control).

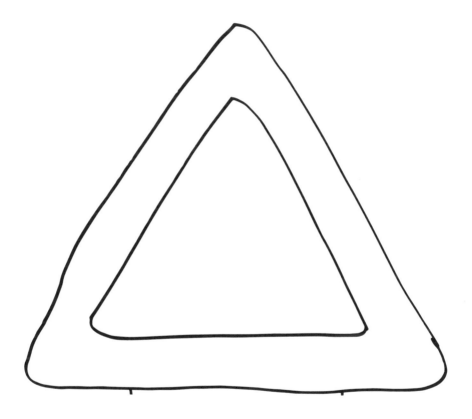

AFFIX IT YOUR DOOR

in extreme circumstances affix it to your person.

Now if you freak out at someone and they get upset it is their own dang fault for not heeding the goddam sign for crissakes

Give your recovery a budget....

MONEY:

(This money is for things like tissues, ice cream and one way tickets to the other side of the world)

TIME:

(Put a reminder in your phone).

cut out and...
PLAY the
SYMPATHY CARD(S)

OFFICIAL SYMPATHY CARD

SYMPATHY REQUIRED

VALID FOR ONE USE ONLY

OFFICIAL SYMPATHY CARD

I deserve hugs

VALID FOR ONE USE ONLY

OFFICIAL SYMPATHY CARD

GIVE ME THAT FOOD

VALID FOR ONE USE ONLY

OFFICIAL SYMPATHY CARD

I already spent that money I owe you, if you care about my feelings you will just drop it.

VALID FOR ONE USE ONLY

OFFICIAL SYMPATHY CARD

I will not be coming in today because my heart has been shattered into a million pieces.

VALID FOR ONE USE ONLY

OFFICIAL SYMPATHY CARD

STOP TALKING AND GO AWAY

VALID FOR ONE USE ONLY

---

once they're gone, they're gone.

HOW HEART-BROKEN ARE YOU?

Please indicate the type and extent of the damage on this heart

STAY ONE STEP AHEAD OF YOUR BRAIN...

Write down the thoughts that your brain is likely to throw at you over the coming months in thought bubbles...

add more thoughts about the thoughts as time goes on

(perhaps you weren't right the first time)

Box off the feelings that those thoughts are likely to cause you

will this change the resultant feelings?

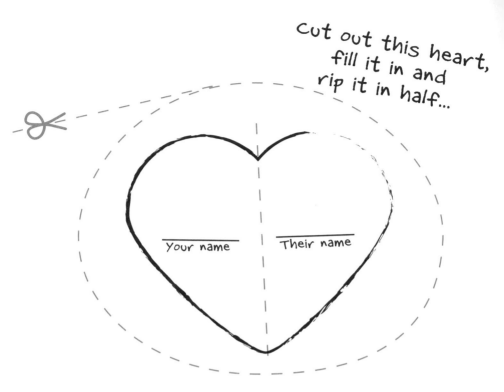

Cut out this heart, fill it in and rip it in half...

Your name | Their name

Write about the emotional repercussions of this simple action

↓

MAKE YOUR OFFICIAL BREAKUP PLAYLIST

choose songs that will help you through the seven stages of grief...

Track 1 (SHOCK): ....

Track 2 (DENIAL): ....

Track 3 (ANGER): ....

Track 4 (BARGAINING): ....

Track 5 (GUILT): ....

Track 6 (DEPRESSION): ....

Track 7 (ACCEPTANCE): ....

CAUTION!

This is your OFFICIAL breakup playlist. These songs will help you NOW but they will forever remind you of your breakup (for all eternity).

CHOOSE WISELY

TOP TIP: Include some Wu Tang

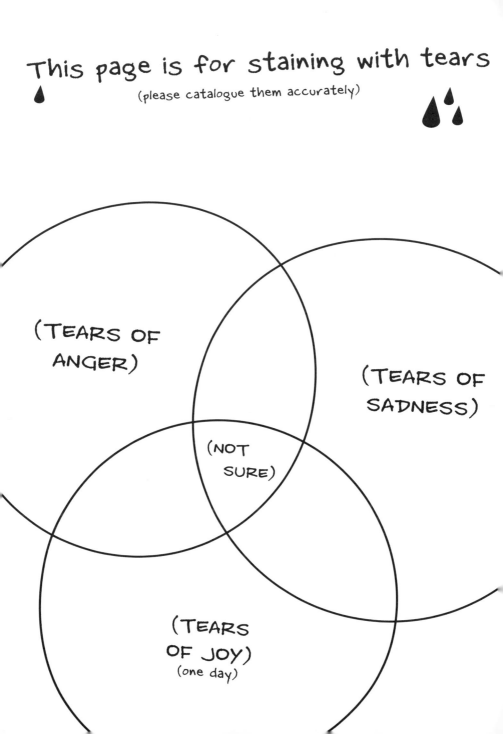

This page is

RESERVED

– for –

TERRIBLE
POETRY
(about your feelings)

let it all out, and then destroy this page
(for humanity's sake)

channel your remaining
emotions into art

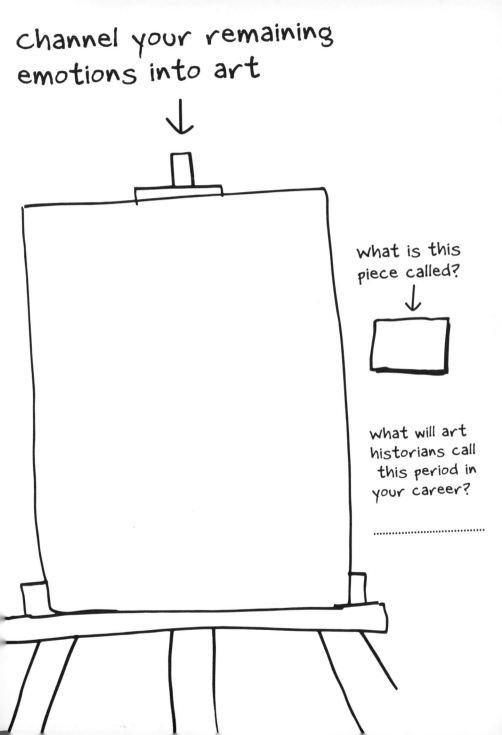

what is this
piece called?

what will art
historians call
this period in
your career?

....

PART 5
COLD TURKEY

write your best friends' numbers here
for emergency complaining purposes

(Including your mum's number is fine)

whenever you get the urge to call
'they-who-shall-not-be-named'
call one of THESE numbers instead

COLD TURKEY CHECKLIST

Tick off everything on this list if you
think a clean break is the only way forward

✓

Tell them what you are doing and why
(keep it brief and don't ask any open questions). ☐

Return anything that belongs to them ☐

Write down their phone number and contact details ☐

Give their contact details to a friend for safe keeping ☐

Delete all of their contact details from your phone ☐

Block them on all social media ☐
(or ask them to block you)

Get rid of all reminders that they were ever in your life

Photos ☐
Videos ☐
Gifts ☐
Letters ☐
Tattoos ☐

If you haven't done them all, you are luke-warm-turkey-ing
(and your goose is cooked)

Are you sure you miss them?
Or are you just horny?

| DEFINITELY MISS THEM | JUST HORNY |

(THINK UP YOUR OWN WAY OF ASSESSING THIS)

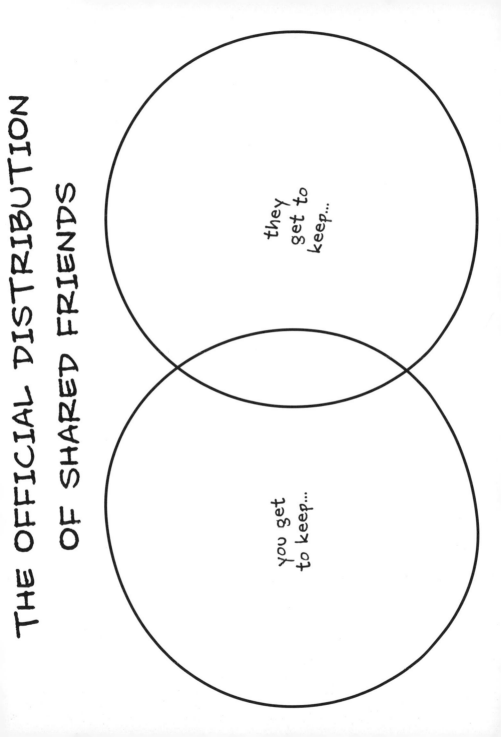

This page represents
YOUR LIFE

The circle represents the giant hole in your life where THEY used to be

FILL THE HOLE WITH
OTHER NEW and FANTASTIC
(non-alcoholic) THINGS

PART 6
THE MORAL HIGH GROUND

The summit of mount innocence

Indicate your relative locations on this moral landscape.

(sea level)

The old abandoned mineshaft of guilt

HOLD YOUR TONGUE!

If things have gotten ugly... write all the horrible stuff you might be tempted to say about that person here to get it out of your system.

Paraphrase everything you've written on the opposite page until it sounds neutral or even complimentary!

You will be sailing above the moral high ground in a hot air balloon of hot air in no time.

PART 7

FIRST ENCOUNTERS

...so you're going
to have to see
them again at

· ·

(even if things are amicable
it's good to be prepared)

SAVING FACE

Fill in the happiness calculators below like so.

THEM

How happy THEY will <u>say</u> they are.

How happy THEY actually are.

YOU

How happy YOU will <u>say</u> you are.

How happy YOU actually are.

– looks like it's time to prepare for –

PSYCHOLOGICAL
WARFARE

strengthen the 'body armour of positivity' with good things you have going on in your life.

shine the 'shield of changing the subject' with alternative, inert conversation topics.

Feed the 'high horse' with things you will NOT gloat about.

sharpen the 'sword of running away to quietly cry in the toilet'

Design yourself a **medal** on this page
(for bravery).

It has been an honour
serving with you.

PART 8
CLOSURE

Write them a
letter and get
EVERYTHING
off your chest.

CLASSIC 'EX—LETTER' STRUCTURE:

Begin by saying how you will always treasure
the memories of the good times to soften
the blow and start on a high note.

THEN... Tell them exactly where they went
wrong and how they ruined your life.

BUT... caveat it by recognizing your own
flaws and explain how you are changing them.

WHILST... subtly hinting that you're dealing
with everything in a really mature way.

DONE?

Good, this letter will no doubt:

- Sort things out entirely
- Be the final word on the matter
- Completely change their mind.
- Make them realize the error of their ways.
- Make you a happier person in the long run.
- Make the world a better place.
- Never be something that you massively regret.

WAIT, on second thoughts
DON'T SEND THIS LETTER!
(Nothing good will come of it)

HAVE A
WORD WITH
YOURSELF

CLOSURE ISN'T A REAL THING

(it's a myth invented by people who like to draw out their pain and have ill-advised sex).

Instead write YOURSELF a letter.

Your FUTURE self.

Write a letter about how you are feeling now, the things you are pissed off about, the things you are looking forward to and the things you hope to achieve over the next few months.

Use these two pages. Use more paper if you have to.

Most importantly, BE HONEST.

(Its only you who will see this).

Dear future _____,

one day this letter will seem hilarious

PART 9
MOVING FORWARD

Draw a light at the end of this tunnel
(choose something you're looking forward to)

make a list of other things that you thought were
cool back in the day that you're totally OVER now.

LAME THINGS THAT I USED TO LIKE....

The way you feel about these things now is how
you will one day feel about your relationship.

GET OVER IT

chart your daily emotional state out of 10 on this 100-day chart. once you are consistently achieving 8s and 9s that's a good sign that you're over 'it'.

10

9

8

- - - - - - - - - - - - - - - -

7

6

5

4

3 < EXAMPLE

2

1

Day 1
Day 2
Day 3
etc

(rock bottom)

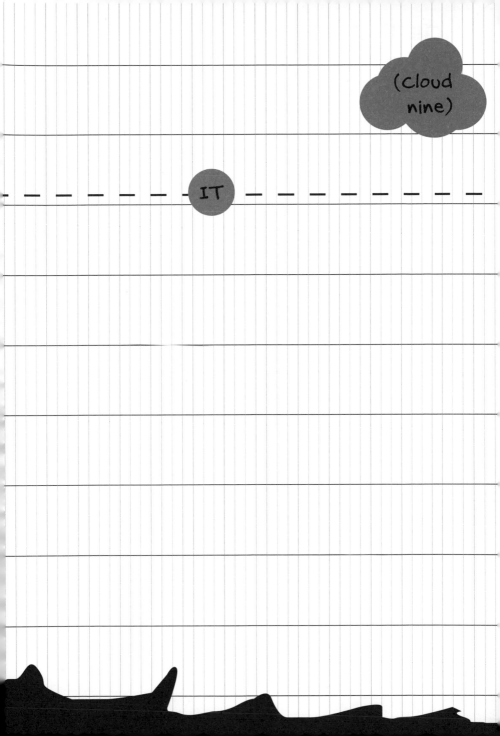

THE BRIGHT SIDE...

Things you have learned about yourself...

Things you have learned about relationships...

Things you have learned about the shared human condition...

Things of theirs you will secretly get to keep...

what new directions have opened up since your breakup?

Has it cleared the way for something else?

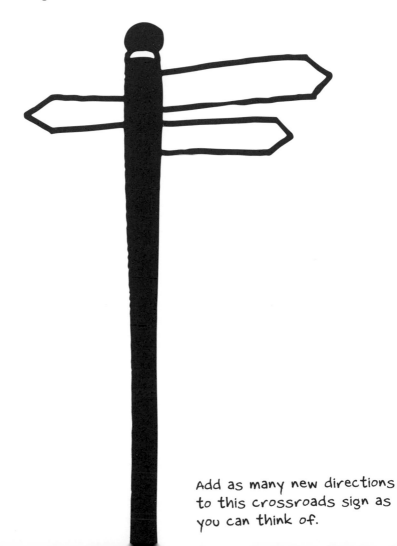

Add as many new directions to this crossroads sign as you can think of.

S O C I A L

Date .... Activity .... With	Date .... Activity .... With	Date .... Activity .... With	Date .... Activity .... With ....
Date .... Activity .... With	Date .... Activity .... With	Date .... Activity .... With	Date .... Activity .... With ....
Date .... Activity .... With	Date .... Activity .... With	Date .... Activity .... With	Date .... Activity .... With ....
Date .... Activity .... With	Date .... Activity .... With	Date .... Activity .... With	Date .... Activity .... With ....

Pick up your phone

and don't put it down until at least five of these boxes are filled in.
(Tea at your granny's house is fine).

L I Z E !

Date .... Activity .... With	Date .... Activity .... With	Date .... Activity .... With	Date .... Activity .... With ....
Date .... Activity .... With	Date .... Activity .... With	Date .... Activity .... With	Date .... Activity .... With ....
Date .... Activity .... With	Date .... Activity .... With	Date .... Activity .... With	Date .... Activity .... With ....
Date .... Activity .... With	Date .... Activity .... With	Date .... Activity .... With	Date .... Activity .... With ....

BY THE WAY

Although it seems like no one will understand how you are feeling and no one wants to hear about your problems, actually opening up to your friends will let them know that you value their opinion and make them feel super important.
SO TALK TO PEOPLE

No ONE change will make you feel better.

Make LOTS of little changes to help you pass the time and jump start the process of moving on.

Get a new haircut ☐

Buy a new outfit ☐

Change up your living space ☐

Confide in someone new ☐

Take a class in something you've never done before ☐

Get a new job ☐

Find a new youtube channel that you're not quite sure how you lived without ☐

Get into yoga ☐

.... ☐

.... ☐

.... ☐

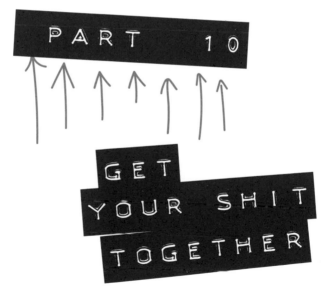

PART 10

GET YOUR SHIT TOGETHER

It's going to be OK

YOU
ARE
HERE
↓

MISERY

Plot your course
to happiness
(feel free to take a few detours)

HAPPINESS

A LIFE OF
BITTER
REGRET

(CAREFUL!)

Write some SHORT-TERM fixes for your day-to-day melancholy on these plasters and indulge yourself to distract from the pain.

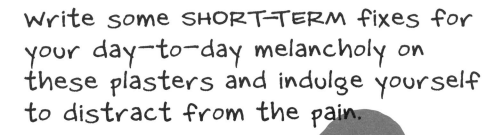

Little treats to look forward to?

Immediate gratification?

Escapism?

A cheeky rebound?

Write yourself a recipe for
LONG-TERM HAPPINESS

INGREDIENTS:

INSTRUCTIONS

The self-esteem train is powered by your own small achievements and nice things you have done for other people. Fill in a bit of track any time you feel you have done something to be proud of (like getting out of bed before noon) and you'll be well on your way to confidenceville station in no time.

THE SELF-ESTEEM TRAIN

confidenceville station

Build a foundation for your future awesomeness
with what you have going for you right now...

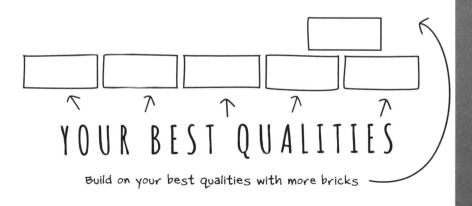

YOUR BEST QUALITIES

Build on your best qualities with more bricks

Let your
VALUES
determine

↓

If I was marooned on a desert island and could only take three things I would take...

1.

2.

3.

If I won a million pounds on the lottery I would...

If I found out I had a month to live I would...

your → **GOALS**

Give your goals a time limit:

I will take the first step by ⋯⋯⋯⋯⋯⋯

I will achieve these goals by ⋯⋯⋯⋯⋯⋯

stop running AWAY from your break-up and
start running TOWARDS your goals

DOODLE A PORTRAIT
of your
BEST POSSIBLE SELF

(make sure it is achievable).

what is different?
Label the diagram.

" search the internet for motivational
quotes and design yourself a poster of
the one that resonates the most.
↓

(put it where you will see it every day)

montage + collage =

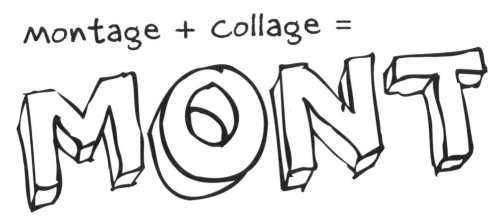

MONT

Take pictures of yourself at the gym or taking piano lessons or grab your receipts for healthy food or whatever and glue them here to make a collage... of your journey to becoming a champion.

Include your sweat if you want this page to be a multi-sensory experience.

LAGE*

* For best results listen to 'Thunder in your Heart' by John Farnham while you make this.

I'm not sure how to say this but...

the new you seems pretty

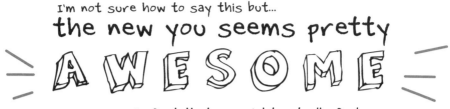

so awesome in fact that you might actually feel
GUILTY about how awesome the new you IS...

Please do the right thing and list some ways you
could hide how great you are now to save your ex
from the trauma of realizing their terrible mistake.

↓

EPILOGUE

make a note of anything of value you have learnt from this life experience so that you may one day help other lost souls overcome the genital-crushingly-high-hurdle that is a break-up when they're in their time of need.

'PSYCHO-EX'-OMETER

Colour in a section on the psycho-ex-ometer for every one of these that you have done...

You still call them by their pet name when you talk.

You say things like 'this is so us'.

You have turned up at their house or work unannounced.

You have called them and hung up.

You have sent them more than three letters.

You send them gifts.

You start trying to hang out with their friends.

You openly jive-talk them on social media.

You smack-talk them to their friends.

You start trying to do the same hobbies as them.

You threaten them in some way.

You appear overly interested in their new partner.

The relationship lasted less than three months and you're reading this book.

This relationship ended over three years ago and you're reading this book.

They have a restraining order against you.

You have boiled their pet.

You have chopped off their penis and thrown it out of a moving vehicle.

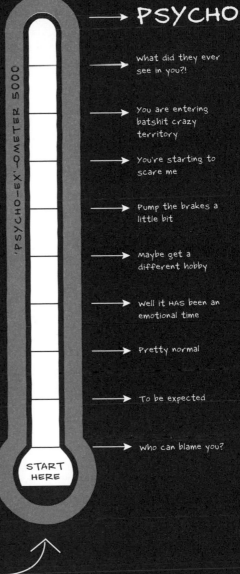

'PSYCHO-EX'-OMETER 5000

FULL BLOWN, OFF-THE-CHART
PSYCHO

What did they ever see in you?!

You are entering batshit crazy territory

You're starting to scare me

Pump the brakes a little bit

Maybe get a different hobby

Well it HAS been an emotional time

Pretty normal

To be expected

Who can blame you?

START HERE

EMERGENCY SECTION

If it has been months and months and you just can't see yourself getting any closer to getting over it...

Take one of the darts that you have been throwing at pictures of your ex and throw it at this page.

wherever it lands...

GO THERE.

(unless it is the sea or a war zone)

(or worse; where you are now).

CONGRATULATIONS!

You have completed the book and successfully

got your shit together

The world is a *brighter* place than you thought, full of POSSIBILITY and WONDER

ONE LAST THING

Rip out the page opposite.

Tear it into tiny pieces to use as kindling and get a fire going in your barbecue/fireplace/fire pit...

BURN THIS BOOK

(and forget you ever needed it)

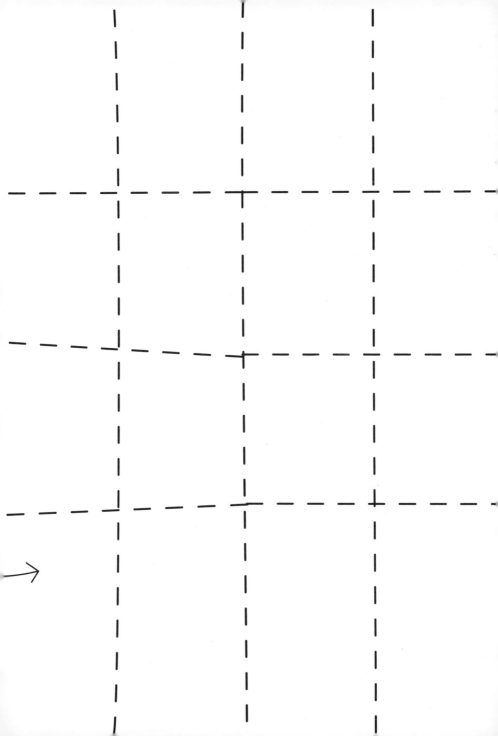

Happy to stay miserable?
This could be the book for you.

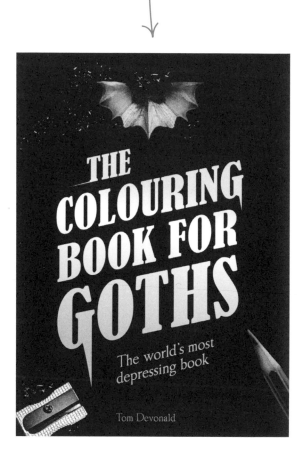